Goldfish

and Other Carp

Editor in Chief: Paul A. Kobasa
Supplementary Publications: Lisa Kwon, Christine Sullivan, Scott Thomas
Research: Mike Barr, Timothy J. Breslin, Cheryl Graham, Barbara Lightner, Loranne Shields
Graphics and Design: Kathy Creech, Sandra Dyrlund, Charlene Epple, Tom Evans
Permissions: Janet Peterson
Indexing: David Pofelski
Prepress and Manufacturing: Anne Dillon, Carma Fazio, Anne Fritzinger, Steven Hueppchen,
    Tina Ramirez
Writer: Alfred J. Smuskiewicz

For information about other World Book publications, visit our Web site at
http://www.worldbook.com or call 1-800-WORLDBK (967-5325).

For information about sales to schools and libraries, call 1-800-975-3250 (United States);
1-800-837-5365 (Canada).

World Book, Inc.
233 N. Michigan Avenue
Chicago, IL 60601
U.S.A.

Library of Congress Cataloging-in-Publication Data

Goldfish and other carp.
    p. cm. -- (World Book's animals of the world)
  Summary: "An introduction to Goldfish and Other Carp, presented in a
highly illustrated, question and answer format. Features include fun
facts, glossary, resource list, index, and scientific classification
list"--Provided by publisher.
  Includes bibliographical references and index.
  ISBN-13: 978-0-7166-1329-9
  ISBN-10: 0-7166-1329-8
  1. Goldfish--Juvenile literature. 2. Carp--Juvenile literature.
I. World Book, Inc. II. Series.
QL638.C94G62 2007
597.484--dc22
                            2006017321

Printed in Malaysia
1 2 3 4 5 6 7 8 09 08 07 06

Picture Acknowledgements: Cover: © Blickwinkel/Alamy Images; © Peter Gathercole, Oxford Scientific/Jupiter Images;
© Gerard Lacz, Animals Animals; © SuperStock; © Gerald D. Tang.

© Blickwinkel/Alamy Images 4, 25, 39; © Brian Bevan, Ardea London 3, 5, 21, 37, 55, 57; © Paul Bricknell, Dorling
Kindersley 59; *Swimming Carp* (ca. 1840) by Utagawa Hiroshige (© Christie's Images/Corbis) 51; © Bogdan Cristel,
Reuters/Corbis 43; © Neil Fletcher, Dorling Kindersley 29; © Peter Gathercole, Oxford Scientific/Jupiter Images 41;
© Altrendo Nature/Getty Images 31; © Larry F. Jernigan, Index Stock/Jupiter Images 53; © DK Images/Index Stock/Jupiter
Images 27; © Gerard Lacz, Animals Animals 45, 47; © M. Loup from Peter Arnold, Inc. 11; © Tim Martin, Nature Picture
Library 49; © Wil Meinderts, Foto Natura/Minden Pictures 5, 13, 47; © Michael Newman, PhotoEdit 17; © Michael Pole,
Corbis 61; © Sami Sarkis, Alamy Images 19; © SuperStock 7; © Gerald D. Tang 15, 23; © David Thompson, OSF/Animals
Animals 35.

Illustrations: WORLD BOOK illustration by John Fleck 9; WORLD BOOK illustrations by Donald Moss 33.

World Book's Animals of the World

Goldfish

and Other Carp

World Book, Inc.
a Scott Fetzer company
Chicago

Contents

What Is a Carp?

Carp are fish—vertebrates *(VUR tuh braytz),* or animals with a backbone, that live in water. Carp are one of the most common types of fish. There are about 2,000 species (kinds) of carp. These different kinds of carp form part of the largest scientific family of freshwater fish (see page 65).

Carp usually are olive-green or yellow-green in color. Many species have whiskers, called barbels. Carp also have forked tails. Most species are covered with scales, but some have few or no scales.

Goldfish belong to the carp and minnow family. In the wild, goldfish generally range in color from olive-brown to bronze or silver. Domestic goldfish—that is, the kinds of goldfish kept by people—consist of about 100 varieties. These goldfish range in color from gold to white, red, black, purple, and yellow.

In addition to goldfish, chubs, dace, and shiners also belong to the carp and minnow family. Fish from this family can live in dirty, murky water—the kind of water that many other fish cannot survive in.

A fantail goldfish

7

What Does a Fish Look Like?

The body of a fish—including a goldfish—resembles that of other vertebrates, or animals with backbones. For example, fish have an internal skeleton, an outer skin, and such internal organs as a heart, intestines, and a brain. In a number of ways, however, a fish's body differs from that of many other vertebrates. For example, instead of legs and arms, a fish has fins that help it to swim and keep its balance. In place of lungs, a fish has gills that allow it to use the dissolved oxygen that exists in water to breathe.

Different breeds of goldfish have different body shapes. Many breeds are streamlined, like a boat. These fish have a small, pointed front and back, with a bigger middle. This shape helps them move through the water easily. Certain other breeds are shaped like an egg.

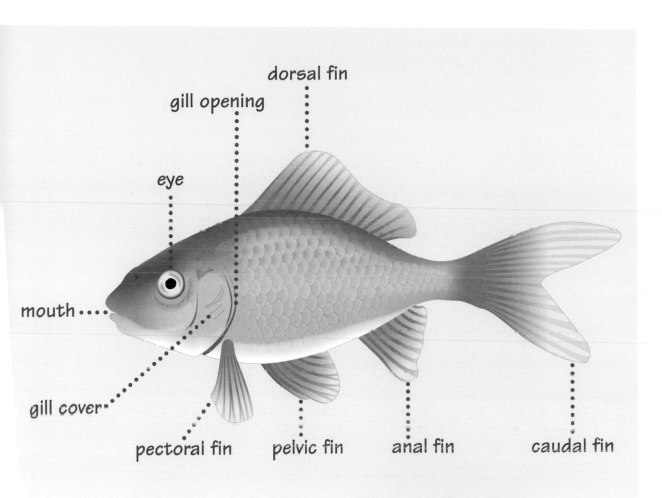

dorsal fin

gill opening

eye

mouth····

gill cover·

pectoral fin

pelvic fin

anal fin

caudal fin

Diagram of a Fish

9

Where Do Goldfish and Other Carp Live in the Wild?

Goldfish are native to China and other parts of Asia, but people have released them in many other areas, including Africa, Australia, Europe, and North America. Goldfish live in both clean and muddy water in all these areas.

Other kinds of carp can also be found around the world in bogs (marshy or swampy areas), creeks, lakes, ponds, rivers, sloughs *(sloos),* and streams. Carp are freshwater fish, so no type of carp lives in the ocean.

Because carp are such hardy, adaptable fish, they are able to survive in many parts of the world.

A carp in the wild

How Did Breeds of Carp, Including Goldfish, Develop?

People have created many breeds of carp. A breed is a group of animals that have the same type of ancestors. Breeds may look different from each other, but they are all in the same species (see page 65). There are more than 125 breeds of goldfish, with such names as comets, shubunkins, and telescopes.

Many breeds of goldfish were developed in China or Japan hundreds of years ago. These breeds were created using a wild species called the Crucian carp.

How do people make new breeds of fish? They first mate unrelated male and female fish that have a little of the desired trait (feature or characteristic), such as fish with speckled colors. If the offspring of these fish have a little more speckling, breeders then mate those fish. Breeders continue this practice, and after several generations (young born to one set of parents at one time), the result may be an all-speckled breed of fish.

Different breeds
of goldfish

What Are Some Unusual Breeds of Goldfish?

There are many unusual breeds of goldfish, with such strange names as the bubble-eye, the celestial, and the pom pom. All three of these fish share one trait that makes them unusual—they all lack a dorsal fin (a fin along the backbone). But, each of these fish has at least one other unusual trait.

When the bubble-eye goldfish is between about 6 and 9 months in age, fluid-filled sacs begin to form around its eyes. By the time the bubble-eye is about 2 years old, these balloonlike sacs can become so large that the fish can have a little difficulty seeing and swimming.

The celestial goldfish has big eyes that bulge out and stare straight up all the time. This breed is also called the stargazer.

The pom pom is named for the big, round bumps above the fish's nose and in front of its eyes. Sometimes the bumps are the same color as the fish's body, but other times the bumps are a different color.

A bubble-eye goldfish

What Should You Look for When Choosing a Goldfish?

When shopping for a goldfish, you first need to find a good pet shop. If you see a lot of dirty tanks or dead fish in a shop, don't try to buy a pet there.

Before you pick a pet goldfish, make sure that the fish is not ill. Here are some signs to watch for:

- When a goldfish is ill, it may gulp air at the surface, swim in a jerky manner, lie on its side, or rub against objects.

- A sick goldfish may also have clouded eyes or fins or gills that are oddly shaped for its breed.

If you buy more than one goldfish, make sure all the fish are about the same size and swim at about the same speed. Bigger, faster fish may harm smaller, slower fish.

Buying goldfish

What Does a Goldfish Eat?

Goldfish are omnivores, which means they eat both animals and plants. Most pet shops sell flaked food made of meat and vegetable matter. As long as this flaked food is made especially for goldfish, it is fine as a basic diet for your pet.

In addition to flaked food, goldfish like to get live food—such as brine shrimp, tubifex worms, or even cut-up earthworms. You can buy these foods at many pet shops. Once in a while, you might give your goldfish such "people" food as boiled spinach, peas, broccoli, or cauliflower.

You should feed your goldfish as much as it will eat in 5 minutes. Goldfish should be fed twice a day.

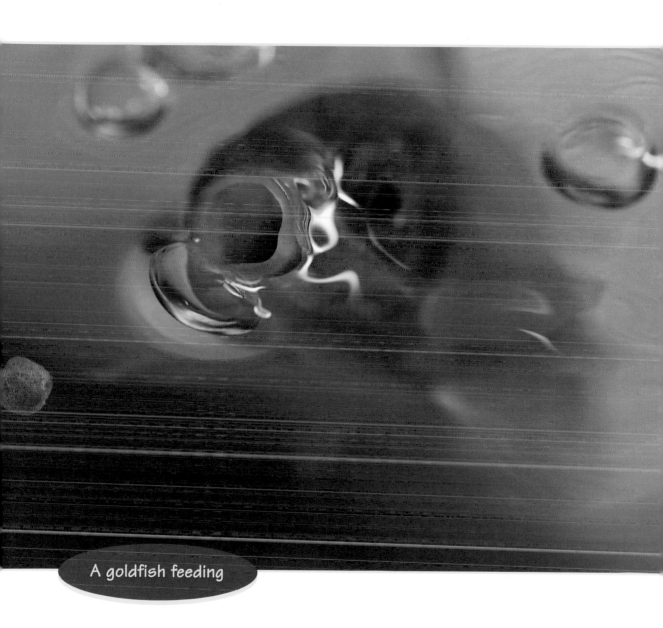

A goldfish feeding

19

Where Should a Pet Goldfish Be Kept?

Pet goldfish can be kept in a small fishbowl, but they will be much better off in a larger tank, called an aquarium *(uh KWAIR ee uhm)*. An aquarium will give your fish more room to swim.

An aquarium should have a cover to keep the fish in and the dirt (and cats) out. It should also have a heater and thermometer to make sure the water stays at a temperature between 65 and 72 °F (18 and 22 °C). Before you add goldfish to your aquarium, let the water stand for 24 hours. This will allow chlorine—a chemical used in small amounts to make water safer for humans—to disappear from the water. Chlorine can harm goldfish.

You should also add a filter, a device that removes dirt from the water, to your aquarium. An air pump will add streams of bubbles to the water to help the fish breathe. An electric light will help you see your fish more clearly. And if you have plants in the aquarium, the light will help them to grow.

Finally, add colorful gravel and fun decorations to your aquarium!

A fully equipped
aquarium

How Do You Keep an Aquarium Clean?

It is important to keep the water and equipment inside your aquarium clean, or your fish may become weak and sick. Cleaning a fish tank or things kept inside that tank, however, should be left to a young adult or adult.

The fish tank filter should be checked once a week to make sure that it is not becoming clogged with dirt or algae (a type of simple life form that grows in many places that have water). The gravel at the bottom of the tank should be stirred up every now and then so that scum doesn't form in it. A buildup of scum in the gravel interferes with water circulation. Special vacuums can be purchased that suction dirt off the gravel and siphon dirty water from the tank.

The water in an aquarium should be changed often to keep it clean. Every week, about one-fourth of the water from a tank should be removed. This water should then be replaced with fresh, new water that has been allowed to sit for 24 hours.

Bacteria that cause an illness called salmonella poisoning are sometimes found in home aquariums. Because of this, a young adult or adult should clean an aquarium. If you touch the water from an aquarium, you should wash your hands with soap and water.

Cleaning an aquarium

Do Goldfish Like Plants?

Goldfish need three main things: oxygen to breathe, food to eat, and shelter to feel safe. Live plants in an aquarium can provide all three of these things.

Plants release oxygen into the water in which they grow. Through a process known as photosynthesis *(FOH toh SIHN thuh sihs),* green plants use sunlight to combine carbon dioxide and water to make food. This process converts light energy into the chemical energy of food. Photosynthesis causes oxygen to be given off into the water by the plants.

Goldfish also can use plants for food. They like to nibble on the leaves of plants.

An aquarium with plants is less stressful for goldfish. If goldfish become frightened, they like to hide behind plants.

Goldfish usually stay healthier and more colorful if plants are in their aquarium. Some easy plants to grow in an aquarium are Java fern, water sprite, sword plant, and banana plant.

A goldfish swims
among plants

How Do Goldfish Breed?

Goldfish become old enough to breed (mate) when they are about 2 years old. Fish breeding is called spawning. During spawning, a male goldfish chases a female for a few hours. If the female becomes ready to mate, she squirts out hundreds of tiny, clear eggs.

The eggs stick to plants and other objects. The male then squirts a substance called milt onto the eggs. Milt fertilizes the eggs, making them grow into new fish.

Neither parent guards the eggs. Parents may even eat their own eggs. If the eggs survive, they usually hatch in about four days.

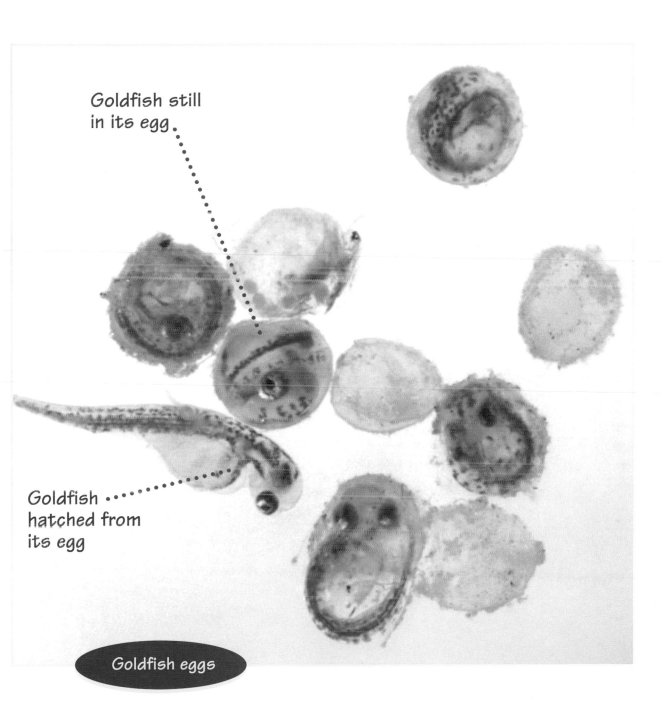

Goldfish still
in its egg

Goldfish
hatched from
its egg

Goldfish eggs

How Can You Care for Goldfish Young?

When you see goldfish eggs, ask an adult to take them out of the aquarium by removing the entire object to which the eggs are stuck. The eggs should then be rinsed in a bucket of clean, chlorine-free water that is the same temperature as the aquarium water. Next, the eggs are placed in a tank with about 6 inches (15 centimeters) of water. A temperature of about 70 °F (21 °C) is best for the water in this small tank.

When the young fish, called fry, hatch out of the eggs, they are $\frac{1}{16}$ to $\frac{1}{8}$ inch (0.16 to 0.32 centimeter) in size—smaller than a letter on this page. The young fish use up their small food supply, called a yolk sac, within a couple days. Then you need to start feeding them.

You can feed goldfish fry various small foods, such as the crushed yolk of a hard-boiled egg, a paste formed from water and oatmeal, or baby brine shrimp. Feed the fry two or three times a day until they are about 4 months old.

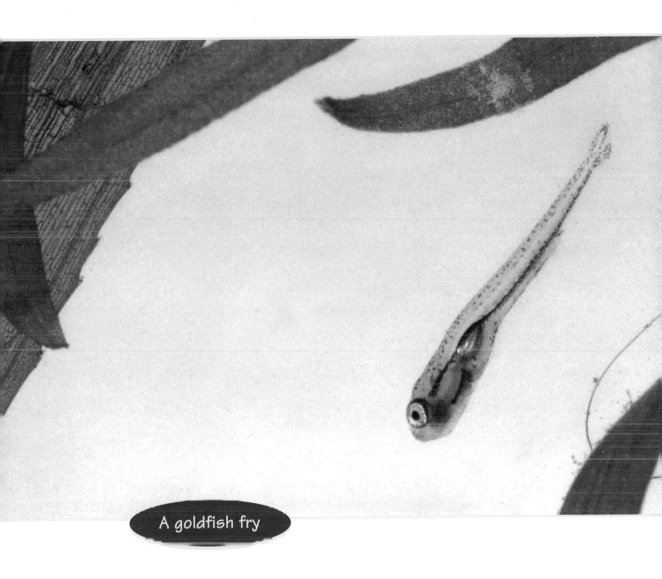

A goldfish fry

Can You Keep Your Goldfish Outdoors?

Indoor aquariums are the best and safest places to keep goldfish. However, certain breeds of goldfish can be kept outdoors in a special ornamental pond. These breeds include common goldfish, comets, and shubunkins. Koi, a type of carp that are closely related to goldfish, are commonly kept in ponds.

A fishpond needs to be at least 2 to 4 feet (61 to 122 centimeters) deep so that the water does not become too hot in summer or too cold in winter. Water lilies grown in the pond will provide shade for the fish.

To help prevent cats, dogs, raccoons, or other animals from catching the fish, a fence should be built all around the pond. And, you should make certain that very small children cannot reach your fishpond and accidentally drown.

In winter in cold areas, some fish can survive in an outdoor pond, providing the pond is not allowed to freeze solid. Many owners, however, find it is easier to bring their fish indoors to an aquarium for the winter.

Goldfish among water lilies in an outdoor pond

What Are Some Other Kinds of Carp?

Goldfish are most people's favorite kind of carp. However, there are hundreds and hundreds of other kinds of carp. Some carp have funny names, such as bonytail, chiselmouth, fathead, hardhead, hornyhead, and stoneroller.

Have you ever gone fishing and used small fish as bait to catch larger fish? The small fish were probably minnows, which belong to the carp and minnow family.

Other kinds of fish in the carp and minnow family include barbs, chubs, dace, danios, and shiners.

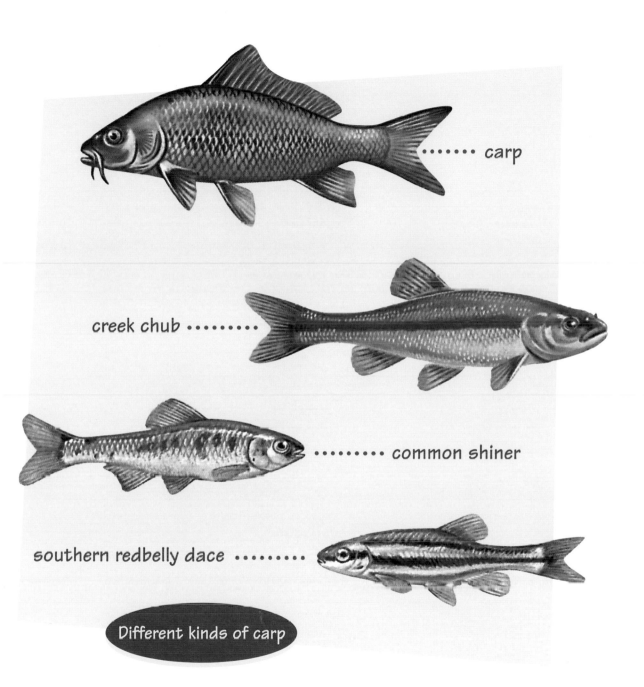

carp

creek chub

common shiner

southern redbelly dace

Different kinds of carp

What Is a Minnow?

A minnow is a kind of carp. Minnows are forage fish. Forage fish furnish the food that allows the game fish sought by anglers (people fishing for sport) to reach a large size. Minnows also are used by anglers as live bait to catch larger fish.

Most American minnows are less than 6 inches (15 centimeters) long. However, some minnows are very large. The Colorado pikeminnow, or squawfish, is a minnow that grows as long as 4 feet (1.2 meters). A minnow called the Indian mahseer grows to 9 feet (2.7 meters) in length.

Two of the more common minnows in the United States and Canada are the brassy minnow and the fathead minnow. Both fish are about 4 inches (10 centimeters) long, and they often live in the same habitats. Fathead minnows are sometimes pond-raised and then sold for bait.

Minnows

What Is a Shiner?

There are many different species of minnows (see page 34) known as shiners (see also page 33). They are called shiners because of their shiny, silvery sides.

Some shiners are brightly colored. Both male and female red shiners are actually silvery-blue, but many male red shiners have red fins and gill openings, especially in the spring. The red shiner is a popular aquarium fish. The golden shiner is the most common baitfish sold in the United States.

At least one type of shiner has an interesting behavior. The male satinfin shiner defends his territory by making knocking sounds when other males get too close. When a male satinfin courts a female, he circles her and makes purring sounds.

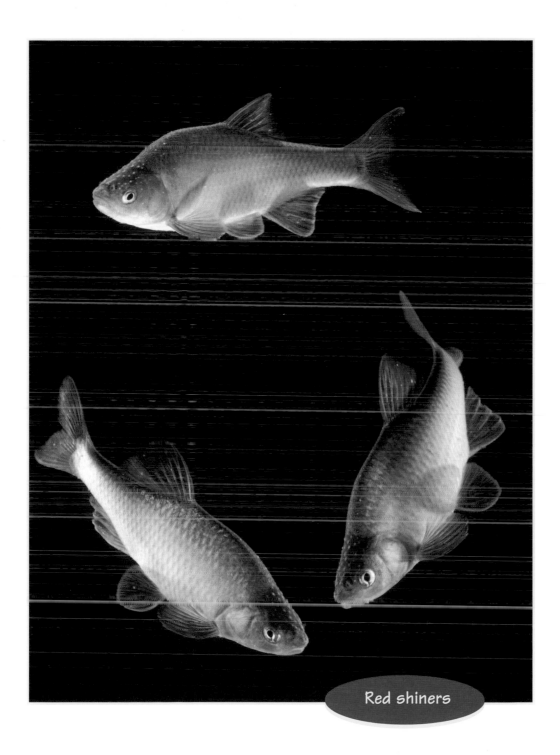

Red shiners

What Is a Dace?

There are various kinds of carp known as dace. Most dace are small fish that are olive-colored above and lighter below. Smallmouth bass and other larger fish like to eat dace.

Two types of dace found in the United States are the southern redbelly dace (see page 33) and the longnose dace. The southern redbelly is about 3 inches (8 centimeters) long and lives in springs and clear streams and ponds, where it often lays its eggs over the gravel nests of other carp. The longnose, which is about 7 inches (18 centimeters) long, lives in similar habitats, but can also be found on lake shorelines.

The common dace is found in Asia and Europe. In some areas of Europe, it is used as a baitfish. This dace can sometimes grow to be as long as 12 inches (30 centimeters).

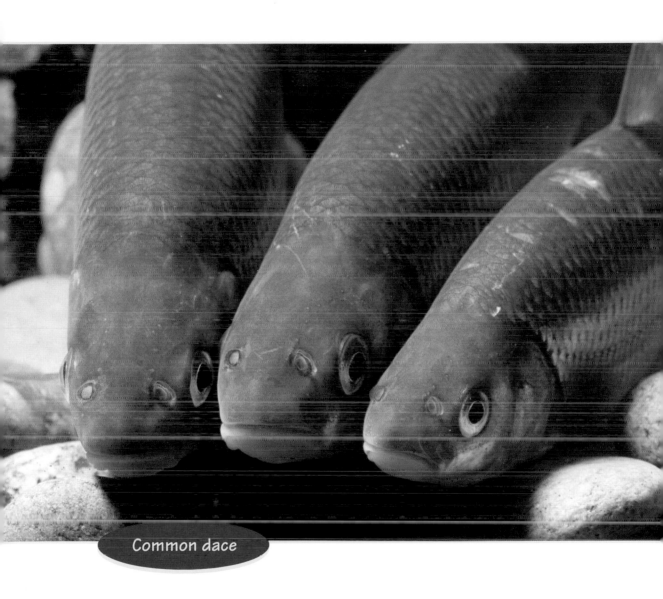

Common dace

39

What Is
a Common Carp?

Growing to a length of more than 30 inches (76 centimeters), the common carp is one of the larger carp species. It can be found in streams, lakes, swampy places or marshy inlets known as sloughs, and other bodies of water from northern Mexico to southern Canada. Common carp eat plants, insects, shellfish, and fish.

The common carp is originally from Europe and Asia. In 1877, the United States government brought large numbers of carp into the United States (see page 46) as a food fish.

Some anglers enjoy fishing for common carp because these fish put up a good fight. Carp fishing is more popular in Europe than in the United States.

A common carp

How Big Do Carp Grow?

With as many as 2,000 species (kinds), carp come in a variety of sizes.

If kept in a large aquarium, some goldfish grow to about 12 inches (30 centimeters) in length. In the wild, some goldfish grow to almost 2 feet (61 centimeters) in length.

Most other kinds of carp are between 12 inches (30 centimeters) and 30 inches (76 centimeters) long and weigh between 2 pounds (0.9 kilograms) and 10 pounds (4.5 kilograms). There are much larger carp, however. The largest species of carp in North America is the Colorado pikeminnow. It can grow to lengths of 3 to 6 feet (0.9 to 1.8 meters).

In 2006, scientists announced that they had discovered the world's smallest fish—a species of carp with a see-through body only about ⅓ inch (8 millimeters) long.

A large carp caught at
a fishing tournament

43

How Long Do Carp Live?

Scientists can tell how old a fish is by counting the growth lines on its scales. These lines are somewhat like the rings on a tree stump—for each year of life, a new line forms.

Goldfish in home aquariums usually live about 5 years, though some have lived for more than 20 years. The oldest known goldfish lived more than 40 years. The better care you give your goldfish, the better are its chances for a long life.

Most wild carp are thought to live between 15 and 18 years. However, this depends on the species. Larger species usually live longer than smaller species.

Goldfish

45

How Did Carp Spread Throughout the United States?

The common carp once lived only in Europe and Asia. In 1877, many of these fish were brought to the United States by the U.S. government. These fish were distributed throughout the country because people thought the common carp was a "miracle fish"—that is, it could be a source of plentiful, inexpensive food for humans. Those original fish and their offspring spread rapidly, and today the common carp lives throughout the United States.

How could a fish species spread throughout a whole country? Besides being released by people in different places, fish can also spread in other ways. For example, fish might swim through streams that connect one body of water with another. Also, ducks or other water birds might carry fish eggs from lake to lake on their feet.

A pair of
common carp

Do Carp Cause Problems?

When hardy species, such as carp, come from other places, they sometimes cause problems for the native animals and plants—that is, the animals and plants that originated there. The native animals and plants are not used to the new species, and they may not have ways to defend against it.

Carp harm many native species of fish by crowding them out of their habitats. Carp also eat the food and eggs of native fish.

Many fishermen in the United States think that carp are a big problem because they pull up the roots of water plants. This stirs up dirt and muddies the water—creating conditions in which other kinds of fish find it difficult to survive.

A carp feeding

What Stories and Legends Are Told About Carp?

Because carp are tough and do well in difficult conditions that would kill other fish, people have made up many stories, legends, and myths about carp. In Asia, carp are used as symbols for certain character traits or abilities that people admire.

In China, carp have long been a symbol of fertility (the ability to produce many young). The Chinese also tell stories of how carp have turned into dragons. In Japan, carp are a symbol of courage and strength. In Korea, carp are a symbol of youth, bravery, strength, and wealth.

A Japanese print
depicting a carp

How Does a Goldfish Know About Its Surroundings?

Goldfish sense their surroundings with sight, smell, and hearing—just like you do.

Because their eyes are positioned at the sides of their head, goldfish see things at the side better than they see things in front of them. They can't close their eyes, because they have no eyelids. Goldfish, therefore, do not like quick changes from darkness to bright light.

Goldfish smell when water carries odors into their nostrils. Although a fish breathes through its gills, it still has nostrils. Water enters and leaves the nostrils of a fish, but the nostrils do not connect to the fish's mouth or throat as they do in humans.

Goldfish do not have external ears. Instead, ear bones inside the head and other structures in the goldfish's body sense vibrations in the water. Goldfish also have special cells on their sides that sense changes in water pressure. Vibrations and pressure changes are what goldfish "hear."

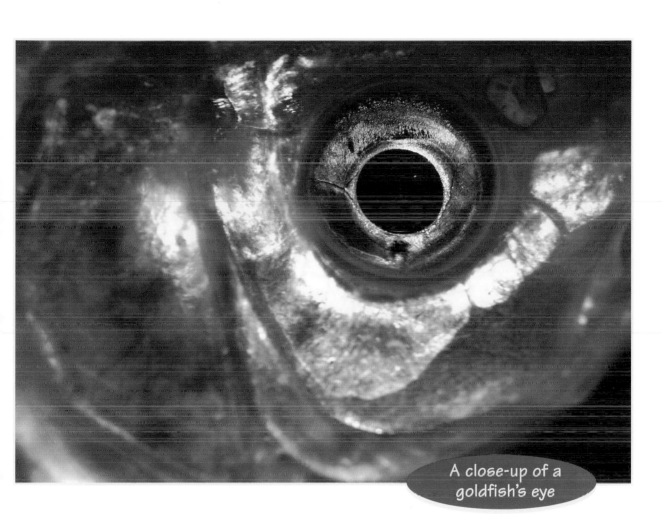

A close-up of a
goldfish's eye

Do Goldfish Sleep?

Have you ever wondered if or how fish sleep? Like other animals, goldfish get tired and they need to rest. Even though they cannot close their eyes, goldfish do sleep.

Goldfish sleep when it is dark. They move around less, and they may sink to near the bottom of the aquarium. They may settle next to a plant or other object for shelter.

Remember to turn the light in your aquarium off at night so that your goldfish can sleep more easily. Fish that are allowed to sleep in the dark at least several hours every night usually do better than fish that do not get to sleep in a darkened tank.

A sleeping goldfish

55

What Are Some Common Signs of Illness in Goldfish?

If your goldfish is not eating or if it is acting strange in other ways, it may be ill.

- If your fish is breathing heavily and rubbing against objects, there may be something wrong with the water—or the fish may have a disease called white spot. This disease is also called ich *(ick).*

- If your goldfish has a soft, yellowish coating on its back, it may have an illness called velvet disease.

- If the fish is shaking its head over and over, it may be trying to shake loose tiny parasites.

- A fuzzy white growth on fins is a sign of a disease called fin rot. A darkening on the skin may be a fungus.

Someone at a pet shop should be able to advise you on remedies that will help your fish. Or ask your veterinarian.

56

Fungus on a goldfish

57

What Routine Veterinary Care Is Needed?

Unlike many other kinds of pets, goldfish do not see a veterinarian once a year to get shots. You can take care of many goldfish health problems by asking an adult to add certain chemicals to your pet's water. Some of these chemicals are added only when your pet shows signs of a disease, but others should be added routinely as a precaution against diseases.

These chemicals may be used to kill disease-causing viruses and microbes (germs), funguses, and other parasites. Some of the things added to aquarium water, however, are used to restore the water to a normal chemical balance.

Ask a veterinarian for further advice about caring for your goldfish.

A veterinarian examining a goldfish

59

What Are Your Responsibilities as an Owner?

If you take good care of your goldfish it is more likely to be a happy, healthy fish that will live a long time. Remember these key things:

- Keep the aquarium water clean.

- Feed your fish the right amount of food.

- Keep the light and temperature of the aquarium at the right levels.

- Watch for signs of illness and make sure that sick fish are quickly treated.

- Take care of any eggs and fry.

- Keep cats and other pets away from your fish.

Finally, enjoy watching your goldfish and learning about its many wild relatives.

Goldfish

Carp Fun Facts

→ By around the A.D. 900's, Buddhist monks in China had built ponds in which to display goldfish.

→ During a single year, a female carp may lay as many as 2 million eggs.

→ The upper jaws of goldfish and other carp can move outward from their skulls to help them pick up bits of food.

→ The jaws of the common carp have no teeth. The fish grinds up food with teeth at the back of its throat.

→ A new goldfish comes out of its egg "tail first."

→ Goldfish grow less brightly colored, or even white, as they age, much as human hair can turn white or gray with age. Sunlight also affects the brightness of a goldfish. It is not the case, however, that a goldfish kept in a darkened room will turn white.

Glossary

barbel A thin, fleshy growth projecting from the mouth or nostrils of certain fish.

bog A marshy or swampy area.

breed To produce animals by carefully selecting and mating them for certain traits. Also, a group of animals or plants having the same type of ancestors.

domestic A tame animal living with or under the care of humans.

dorsal fin A fin or finlike part on the back of some fish.

freshwater Of or living in water that is not salty.

fry Young fish.

gill A feathery, blood-filled organ that some animals use to take in oxygen from the surrounding water.

habitat The area where an animal lives, which contains everything the animal needs to survive.

milt The sperm cells of male fish, including the milky fluid that contains these cells.

omnivore An animal that eats both animals and plants.

slough A swampy place or marshy inlet.

spawning The process whereby animals that grow or live in water, such as fish and frogs, produce eggs.

species A group of animals that have certain permanent characteristics in common and are able to produce offspring.

trait Features or characteristics particular to a breed.

vertebrate An animal with a backbone and a skull enclosing the brain.

63

Index

For more information about Goldfish and Other Carp, try these resources:

The Essential Goldfish, by Maddy Hargrove, Howell Book House, 1999

Goldfish: A Complete Pet Owner's Manual, by Marshall E. Ostrow, Barron's Educational Series, 2003

I Am Your Goldfish, by Gill Page, Waterbird Press, 2004

http://animaldiversity.ummz.umich.edu/site/accounts/information/Carassius_auratus.html
http://www.cnr.vt.edu/efish/families/cyprinidae.html
http://www.kokosgoldfish.com/

Carp Classification

Scientists classify animals by placing them into groups. The animal kingdom is a group that contains all the world's animals. Phylum, class, order, and family are smaller groups. Each phylum contains many classes. A class contains orders, an order contains families, and a family contains genuses. One or more species belong to each genus. Each species has its own scientific name. (The abbreviation "spp." after a genus name indicates that a group of species from a genus is being discussed.) Here is how the animals in this book fit into this system.

Animals with backbones and their relatives (Phylum Chordata)
Bony fish (Class Osteichthyes)
Ray-finned fishes (Subclass Actinopterygii)
Carp and their relatives (Order Cypriniformes)

Carp and minnows (Family Cyprinidae)

Domestic goldfish	*Carassius auratus*
Crucian carp, or wild goldfish	*Carassius carassius*
Chiselmouth	*Acrocheilus alutaceus*
Barbs	*Barbus* spp.
Indian mahseer minnow	*Barbus tor*
Stonerollers	*Campostoma* spp.
Satinfin shiner	*Cyprinella analostana*
Red shiner	*Cyprinella lutrensis*
Common carp	*Cyprinus carpio*
Danios	*Danio* spp.
Bonytail	*Gila elegans*
Brassy minnow	*Hybognathus hankinsoni*
Common dace	*Leuciscus leuciscus*
Common shiner	*Luxilus cornutus*
Hardhead	*Mylopharodon conocephalus*
Hornyhead chub	*Nocomis biguttatus*
Golden shiner	*Notemigonus crysoleucas*
Southern redbelly dace	*Phoxinus erythrogaster*
Fathead minnow	*Pimephales promelas*
Colorado pikeminnow, or Colorado squawfish	*Ptychocheilus lucius*
Longnose dace	*Rhinichthys cataractae*
Creek chub	*Semotilus atromaculatus*